HUGHES

W9-AYV-969

DK **Watch me grow**

Butterfly

LONDON, NEW YORK, MUNICH,
MELBOURNE and DELHI

Written and edited by Lisa Magloff
Designed by Sonia Whillock,
Mary Sandberg, and Pilar Morales
Additional Digital Artwork by Darren Jordan

Publishing Manager Sue Leonard
Managing Art Editor Clare Shedden
Jacket Design Simon Oon
Picture Researcher Cynthia Frazer
Production Shivani Pandey
DTP Designer Almudena Díaz

First American Edition, 2003

Published in the United States by
DK Publishing Inc.
375 Hudson Street
New York, NY 10014

A Cataloging-in-Publication record for this book
is available from the Library of Congress.

ISBN 0-7566-0193-2

Color reproduction by
Media, Development and Printing, Ltd., Great Britain
Printed and bound by
South China Printing Co, Ltd., China

Discover more at
www.dk.com

Come fly with us and

Contents

watch us GROW!

I'm a butterfly

I use my colorful wings
to fly from flower to flower,
and drink nectar through
my long, curly tongue.

Its body is
covered with
millions of
soft hairs.

Antennae help
the butterfly
to smell and
to balance.

The butterfly sucks
nectar through its hollow
proboscis, which uncurls
to act like a straw!

4

This is a close-up of my scales.

A butterfly's wings are made up of thousands of tiny scales.

Now turn the page and watch me GROW!... 5

Before I was born

Mom and Dad met while they were flying in a field. They flew around each other for a few minutes, and then landed on a flower to mate.

After mating, the male flies away and the female looks for a plant where she can lay her eggs.

Egg laying

The female curves her bendy body towards a leaf to lay her eggs. The eggs are sticky so they don't roll away.

Home sweet home

Each type of butterfly will lay its eggs on only a few plants. The type of butterfly in this book likes carrot and fennel plants best.

Giant fennel

wild carrot

Time to hatch

After about five days of growing inside my egg, I am ready to hatch out as a tiny caterpillar. I have to chew my way out of my egg. It's hard work.

This two-day-old egg will soon start to change color.

It takes many hours for the caterpillar to chew its way out of the egg.

Home sweet home
Butterflies live just about anywhere there are flowers. Spring is the best time to find their tiny eggs, but you have to look very carefully.

My eggshell is my first meal!

9

I am growing bigger

The more I eat, the bigger I get. Soon, I can't fit into my skin any more. It's time for me to shed my old skin and grow a bigger skin. Each skin is a different color.

7 days   **12 days**   **18 days**

Sometimes the caterpillar eats its old skin after shedding.

Danger alert
When the caterpillar senses danger, this orange scent horn pops up and gives off a stinky odor to scare away enemies.

10

Caterpillars do not have lungs. Instead, they breathe through holes in their skin.

I'm very hungry

This three-week-old caterpillar has to eat all the time. It has only a few weeks to store enough energy to change into a butterfly.

These are my teeth!

I don't sleep, I just eat, and eat, and eat.

Sharp spikes warn other animals to stay away.

Munch, crunch!

Caterpillars have lots of feet so they can grip on to branches.

Crunchy facts

🦋 Caterpillars are fussy eaters. Most eat only one or two kinds of plant.

🦋 If you grew as fast as a caterpillar, you would be as big as a truck in two weeks!

13

Holding on tight

After about four weeks I find a nice, strong branch and spin some sticky silk thread to help me hang on. Now I'm ready to shed my skin for the last time.

The pad of coiled thread on my tail is called the pillow.

It's time to begin the change into a butterfly.

The thread around the caterpillar's middle is called the belt.

The caterpillar sheds its skin. Underneath, a shell has formed.

The shell will harden into a protective case called a chrysalis.

Inside, the caterpillar turns into a lump of soft, squishy jelly.

15

Time to break out

It's been almost three weeks since I started changing. The soft jelly inside my chrysalis is turning into the body of a beautiful butterfly.

See-through package
When it is time to hatch, the chrysalis turns clear. Look closely. Can you see the color of the new butterfly?

I push and I shove and my chrysalis splits open.

16

When the butterfly emerges, its wings are wet and crumpled.

Hatching facts

🦋 Some butterflies spend the winter in their chrysalis, then hatch in the spring.

🦋 A butterfly's skeleton is on the outside of its body to protect it.

The butterfly pumps blood into its wings to help them expand.

Get ready to fly

It only takes a few minutes
for my wings to dry off.
Now I am ready to
look for flowers,
which is where
I will find my
new food.

The empty chrysalis
is left behind.

My wings are dry and I'm ready to fly.

18

The adult butterfly
will live for about a
month, so there is
not much time
to find a mate.

Slurp Slurp
From now on, the butterfly
will drink nectar through
its tongue, or proboscis.

19

The circle of life goes round and round.

Now you know how I turned into a beautiful butterfly.

Bye bye, I'm off in a flutter!

My friends from around the world

To scare off birds, the Peacock Butterfly has spots that look like eyes.

Can you find me?

This Leaf Butterfly hides by looking like a dead leaf.

I'm a Pygmy Butterfly and I'm the smallest!

The Clubtail Butterfly lives in warm, wet rain forests.

I'm the biggest. This pale green

22

My butterfly friends around the world come in all the colors of the rainbow.

This butterfly from South America is called the 88 Butterfly. Can you see why?

The Blue Morpho Butterfly likes to drink the juice of rotting fruit.

The Malachite Butterfly eats bird droppings!

The Queen Alexandra Butterfly comes from New Guinea.

shape shows my real size.

Butterfly facts

🦋 Monarch Butterflies travel 4,000 miles (8,800 km) each year, from the Great Lakes to the Gulf of Mexico and back.

🦋 There are about 28,000 different types of butterfly.

🦋 A butterfly cannot fly if its body temperature falls below 86° F (30° C).

Glossary

Proboscis
The butterfly uses this part of its body to drink nectar.

Shedding
The caterpillar loses its old skin and grows bigger skin.

Hatching
When the baby caterpillar first comes out of its egg.

Chrysalis
The stage when the caterpillar is changing into a butterfly.

Caterpillar
The second stage of a butterfly's life cycle, after egg.

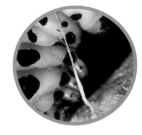
Silk
The thread the caterpillar makes to hold it onto a branch.

Acknowledgments
The publisher would like to thank the following for their kind permission to reproduce their photographs: Jerry Young, Andy Crawford, Frank Greenaway, Colin Keates, Natural History Museum, Derek Hall, Eric Crichton, Kim Taylor, Jane Burton (Key: a=above; c=center; b=below; l=left; r=right; t=top)
1: Alamy Images t; 2-3: N.H.P.A./Laurie Campbell b; 3: Oxford Scientific Films/Stan Osolinski tr; 4: Duncan McEwan/naturepl.com clb; 4-5: Oxford Scientific Films/Raymond Blythe; 5: Science Photo Library/Andrew Syred tl; 6-7: Flowerphotos/Carol Sharp; 6: Richard Revels; 7: Corbis/George McCarthy (butterfly) ca; 7: Windrush Photos/Richard Revels (leaf & egg) ca; 8-9: FLPA - Images of nature/Ian Rose (background); 8-9: Windrush Photos/Richard Revels c; 9: Woodfall Wild Images/Richard Revels b; 10: Ardea London Ltd/Pascal Goetgheluck clb;

10-11: Oxford Scientific Films/Raymond Blythe; 12-13: FLPA - Images of Nature/Ian Rose (background); 12-13: Hans Christoph Kappel/naturepl.com (caterpillar); 12: N.H.P.A./Daniel Heuclin cra; 14-15: Richard Revels (caterpillar); 15: Richard Revels tr, cr, br; 16: Richard Revels cla, bc; 17: Richard Revels; 18: Richard Revels; 19 Ingo Arndt/naturepl.com r; 20: FLPA - Images of nature/Roger Wilmshurst c; 20: Hans Christoph Kappel/naturepl.com tl; 20: Richard Revels cla, clb, bcl; 21: Sonia Halliday Photographs/Sister Daniel (background); 21: Hans Christoph/naturepl.com c; 24: Ardea London Ltd/Ian Beames br; 24: Oxford Scientific Films/Raymond Blythe tr.

All other images © Dorling Kindersley
For further information see: www.dkimages.com

MARY FRANK SCHOOL LIBRARY

T 7718

E   Kraus, Robert
Kra
            Kittens for nothing

Kittens for Nothing

Kittens for Nothing
by Robert Kraus · illustrated by Diane Paterson

Windmill Books, Inc.
and E. P. Dutton & Co., Inc.
New York

Text copyright © 1976 by Robert Kraus
Illustrations copyright © 1976 by Diane Paterson
All rights reserved
Published by Windmill Books & E.P. Dutton & Co.
201 Park Avenue South, New York, New York 10003

LIBRARY OF CONGRESS CATALOGING IN PUBLICATION DATA

Kraus, Robert   Kittens for nothing.

SUMMARY: It seems the children will never get rid of the
nine kittens when they can't sell or even give them away.

(1.)Cats—Fiction) I. Paterson, Diane II. Title.
PZ7. K868Ki (E) 75-25980 ISBN 0-525-61538-5

Published simultaneously in Canada by Clarke,
Irwin & Co., Limited, Toronto and Vancouver

Printed in the U.S.A.   First Edition
        10 9 8 7 6 5 4 3 2 1

For Pamela, Bruce, Billy,
Betsy, Jana, and Robert

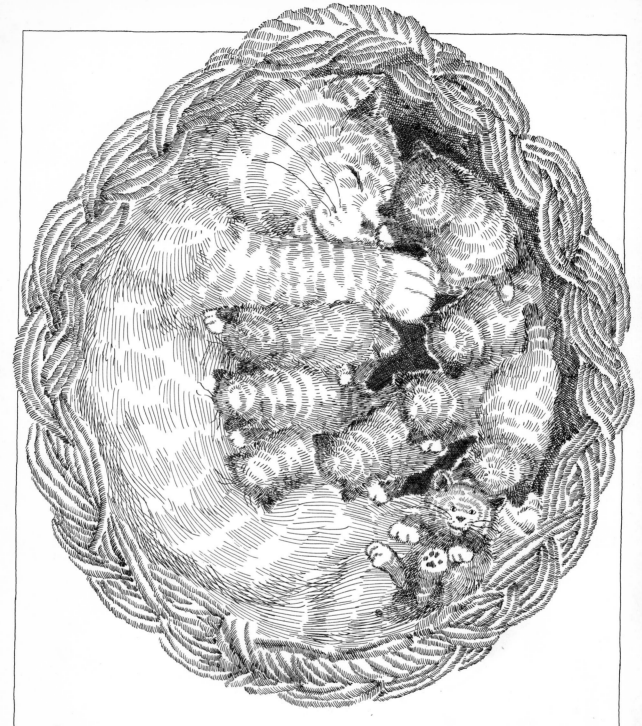

Mittens had nine kittens, which are nine kittens too many. Especially when the father of the house is allergic to even one cat.

So the children decided to *sell* the kittens.

Many people passed and some stopped an

dmired the kittens. But nobody bought any.

Kittens for Sale

"We must be doing something wrong," said the children. So the boy changed the sign to read "Kittens for Nothing." That ought to do it, they thought.

Kittens for

But it **didn't** do it. More people passed and some stopped and admired the kittens. But nobody took a kitten, even for nothing.

Kittens for Sale
Nothing

"We've got to do something," said the boy. "That's for sure," said the girl. So they put the kittens in a basket and put the basket in a wagon and decided to try to give them away door to door.

Kittens for ~~Sale~~ Nothing

They rang the door bell of a neat house. A neat lady opened the door. "Kittens for nothing?" asked the children. "Kittens make messes," said the neat lady. "I wouldn't take those kittens if you paid me." "We hadn't thought of that," said the children.

So they rang the bell of the house next door.
A mouse answered. When he saw the
basket of kittens he shut the door quickly.

So the children rang the bell of the house next door. A plump, rumpled man with a parakeet on his head opened the door.
"Kittens for nothing?" said the children.
"Kittens would eat my parakeet," said the rumpled man, taking the parakeet off of his head and giving it a kiss.
"I guess so," said the children.

Kittens for Sale
Nothing

So the children rang the bell of the next house. They rang and rang but nobody answered. "Nobody home," they said. They were very discouraged. They couldn't take the kittens back home because their father was so allergic he would sneeze himself silly. And they couldn't sell the kittens or even give them away. "I wish Mittens had never had them," said the children.

Kittens for

Sale
Nothing

There was one more house on the block. It had an iron fence around it and was dark and forbidding. The children were frightened, but could leave no stone unturned or doorbell unrung.

Trembling just a little, they rang the doorbell. The front door creaked open and an old lady peeked out at them but said not a word. "K-k-kittens for nothing?" said the children.

"Kittens?" said the old lady. "Did you say kittens?" "Yes," said the children.

"If you think **you** have kittens, come inside and see **my** kittens!" She flung open the door.

"You have more cats than you need," said the boy. "So I guess you don't want our kittens for nothing." "That's what you think," said the old lady. "The more cats the merrier! That's my motto."

So the children gave the old lady the nine kittens for nothing and a better home for them could not have been found. "You may visit them whenever you like," said the old lady. "We will," said the children.

And they did. And some days they brought Mittens along.